GOD SPEAKS TO HIS CHILDREN

Texts from the Bible

This edition was commissioned by
the International Catholic Charity
«Aid to the Church in Need»

3｜ ）
paña

AID TO THE CHURCH IN NEED
124 Carshalton Road
Sutton
Surrey SM1 4RL
Tel. 081-642-8668

Front cover:
The son that was lost (No. 73)

Back cover:
The Flight to Egypt (No. 50)
The Transfiguration (No. 67)
Jesus raises to life the son of the widow from Nain (No. 62)
The Last Supper (No. 80)

Text: *Eleonore Beck*. Illustrations: *Miren Sorne*. All rights reserved: © *Kirche in Not, Postfach 1209, D-6240-Königstein, Federal Republic of Germany,* © *Editorial Verbo Divino, 1990. Cum licentia ecclesiastica. Printed in Spain. Photocomposition: Cometip, S.L., Plaza de los Fueros, 4. 31010 Barañain (Navarra). Printing: Mateu Cromo, S.A., 28320 Pinto (Madrid).*

Depósito Legal: M. 12.234-1990

ISBN: 84-7151-661-6

Edición en Inglés (Bi/1)

FROM THE BOOKS
OF THE OLD TESTAMENT

THE BEGINNING

1. God creates the world

In the beginning God created heaven and earth. The earth was waste and empty. But God's Spirit hovered over the waters.

God said: Let there be light! And there was light. God saw that the light was good. God separated the light from the darkness. He said to the light: You are day. To the darkness he said: You are night. It was the first day.

God said: Let clouds gather up above. Let rain

from them fall on the earth. God said to the skies above: You are heaven. It was the second day.

God said: Let the waters gather together, so that dry land appears. God said to the dry land: you are earth. To the waters gathered below he said: You are the sea. And God saw that earth and sea were good.

God said: Let the earth bring forth all kinds of plants and trees. The plants sprouted up and grew green. God saw that it was good. It was the third day.

God said: Let there be lights in the heavens. The sun during the day, the moon and the stars at night. Let them show the times: day and night, week and month, and the seasons. God saw that it was good. It was the fourth day.

God said: Let fish swim in the water. Let birds fly over the earth. Let all kinds of animals, great and small, live on the land. And so it happened. God saw that it was good. It was the fifth day.

God said: Let us make man in our own image and likeness. I will entrust the earth to them: all the fishes, birds, animals and plants. God created man in his own image. As male and female he created them. He blessed them and said: Be fruitful and multiply. I entrust the earth to you. You are more than the fish, the birds, the animals and the plants. You are to care for them. The plants are to serve as food for you and the animals. God saw everything that he had made; it was very good. It was the sixth day.

God created the universe in six days: heaven, earth, sea and all living things. On the seventh day God rested. So the seventh day is a blessed and holy day for man. (Gen 1)

2. God grants man Paradise

God formed the first man, Adam, out of earth from the field and breathed into him his breath of life. Thus man became a living being.

Then God planted a garden in Eden. He caused many kinds of trees to grow. It was good to see them and their fruit was delicious. In the middle of the garden grew the tree of life and the tree of the knowledge of good and evil.

God brought the man he had made into the garden, so that Adam might cultivate and look after it. He said to the man: You may eat the fruit of all the trees in the garden. It is only the fruit of the tree of knowledge of good and evil that you may not eat. If you eat its fruit, you will have to die.

God did not want the man to remain alone. So God brought all the animals and birds to Adam and he gave them their names. However, he did not find one that was really suited to him. So God made the man fall into a deep sleep. He took one of Adam's ribs and formed it into a woman. When Adam saw her, he said: She is as I am. Let her name be woman, because she was taken from me. The man and the woman were naked. But they felt no shame in front of each other. (Gen 2)

3. Mankind loses Paradise

The man and the woman lived in the garden that God had entrusted to them. There was enough to eat. They lived in peace with the animals. They were happy, since God was their friend. Everything was good. But then the serpent said to the woman: Did God really forbid you to eat from any of the trees in the garden? The woman replied: Not at all! We may eat the fruit of all the trees in the garden, except for the one in the middle of the garden. We may not eat its fruit, otherwise we shall die. But no, said the serpent. You will not die. On the contrary, your eyes will be opened. You will know what is good and what is evil - just like God.

The woman saw that the fruit of the tree was delicious to eat and could make them wise. She took and ate. And she gave some to her husband to eat. Then their eyes were opened. They realised that they were naked. So they sewed loin-cloths out of fig leaves. In the evening they heard God's footsteps in the garden. They hid themselves. But God called out to the man: Where are you? Adam answered: I heard your footstep. I was afraid. I hid myself because I am naked. God asked: How do you know that? Have you eaten of the tree from which I have forbidden you to eat? Adam passed the blame onto the woman: She gave me the fruit to eat. And the woman blamed the serpent: It tempted me.

God said to the serpent: Because you have done this, you are accursed. You shall crawl on your belly and eat dust. The woman will be your enemy. Her children will be the enemy of your children. They will crush your head and you will bite their heel.

God said to the woman: It will be hard for you. You will bear your children in pain. God said to the man: You have broken my commandment. You will see that the earth is not paradise. You will have to work hard until you die, so that you and your family

do not go hungry. Then you will return to the earth from which I formed you.

Adam called his wife Eve, which means: life. She became the mother of all those who live. The Lord God expelled the man and the woman from paradise. His guard, with a sword of flame, kept watch over the entrance and over the path to the tree of life. (Gen 3)

4. Cain and Abel

Adam and Eve had two sons: Cain and Abel. Abel became a shepherd, Cain tilled the soil. He brought some of the corn in his fields as a thanksgiving offering to God. Abel offered one of his best lambs. God was pleased with Abel's offering. He did not look with favour on Cain's offering. This made Cain angry and bitter. God warned him: Why are you angry? Why are you staring in front of you? If you are planning good, you can look everybody in the eye. If you are planning evil, then sin is lying in wait for you. It wants to devour you, but you can master it.

7

Cain said to his brother: Come out with me into the field. When they were out in the field, Cain killed his brother. God asked Cain: Where is Abel, your brother? Cain replied: I do not know. Am I my brother's guardian? Then God said to him: What have you done? Your brother's blood has flowed into the earth. You cannot remain a tiller of the soil because the earth will no longer bear fruit for you. You have lost your homeland. From now on you must wander from place to place without rest.

Cain complained: My punishment is too great. You are driving me from the soil and out of Your presence. You are making me a homeless wanderer. Anyone can kill me. So, God put a mark on Cain's forehead to protect him. (Gen 4, 1-15)

5. Noah and the great flood

God saw that the men he had created in his image were growing more and more evil in their thoughts and deeds. The earth was full of violence. So God regretted having made man. He said: I will wipe the men I have created from the face of the earth; the men, the animals and everything living on earth.

Noah had remained faithful to God. So God wanted to save him from the coming judgement. God said to Noah: Make an ark out of wood, that can float on water like a big ship. Then I will send a mighty flood over the earth. All living things will perish in the water. Only you and those with you in the ark will be saved.

Noah began to build an ark with his sons, just as God had said. They built many rooms in the ship because they were to take a pair of every kind of animal with them. God had told them to. When the ark was ready, Noah gathered supplies. Then he boarded the ark with his sons and their families. They took one pair of each kind of animal with them. God himself closed the door behind them.

Then it began to rain. Water poured down from heaven and flooded the earth. It rose higher and higher. The animals drowned - and the men also. The birds found no tree to perch on. Thus all living things on earth drowned. Only Noah and those with him in the ark survived the flood.

Finally, after forty long days, the rain stopped. When the water began to go down, Noah first let out a raven. It soon returned to him. Then, a week later, he released a dove. It also returned. Finally, a second dove, which Noah let fly a week later, brought an olive branch back to the ark in its beak. Soon after, God said to Noah: Now you can come out. You and all who were saved with you. They came out of the ark. The men and the animals. A new life began for all of them. Noah thanked God and offered him a sacrifice.

God spoke to Noah: I will establish my Covenant for you, for the men and the animals. You and your children can live under this Covenant. I also promise that I will never again send a flood to destroy life on earth. (Gen 6-9)

THE PATRIARCHS

6. God calls Abraham

Abraham was a shepherd. God spoke to him: Go! Leave your homeland, your relatives and your father's house. Enter the land that I will show you. I will make you into a great nation. I will bless you and make your name famous. In you all men will see what it means to be blessed. I will wish well to all those who wish you well; I will curse all those who wish you evil. All men will be blessed through you.

Abraham set out as God had bidden him. He was seventy-five years old. He took with him his wife Sa-

rah, his nephew Lot, all the animals that belonged to
him and all those who worked for him. Abraham
entered the land that God had promised him and his
children. It was a good and fruitful land, the land of
Canaan. There Abraham built altars for God. (Gen 12,
1-8)

7. God's promise to Abraham

One night God spoke with Abraham. He said: Do
not be afraid! I will protect you and make you rich.
Abraham replied: How can riches mean anything to
me as long as you deny me what is most important? I
have no son to be my heir and pass on my name. So
God led Abraham outside the tent: Look up to heaven.
See the stars. That is how many sons and daughters
you will have. Abraham trusted God and God recognised Abraham's faith.

Abraham had pitched his tent near the oaks of
Mamre. About noon he sat in the entrance of the tent.
There he saw three men coming towards him. Abra-
ham stood up and ran to meet them: Do not pass me

by. Come and rest. Abraham gave the strangers butter and milk, meat and bread to eat. After the meal one of the guests asked Abraham: Where is your wife Sarah? She is in the tent, replied Abraham. The stranger said: Next year about this time I will come again and Sarah will have a son.

Sarah stood behind Abraham in the tent. She heard what the stranger said. She laughed and thought to herself: The stranger probably does not know how old I am. Abraham is also an old man. But the stranger asked: Is anything impossible for God? (Gen 15, 1-8; 18)

8. Abraham's faith

God kept his promise. Sarah, an old woman, became a mother. Abraham, an old man, became a father and acquired an heir. Sarah and Abraham gave their son the name that God himself had chosen for him: Isaac, which means: May God smile. Isaac grew up into boyhood.

God wanted to test Abraham. He said to him: Take your son, your only son, whom you love, and offer him to me as a burnt sacrifice. The next morning Abraham fetched his donkey and loaded it with wood. Then he called his servants and his son. They travelled for three days until they reached a mountain. There Abraham left his servants and the donkey. Stay here, he told them. Isaac will go with me up the mountain. We will return when we have prayed and offered sacrifice.

Isaac carried the wood. Abraham carried the knife and the pot with the glowing coals. Father, said Isaac, we have wood and fire, but no lamb to sacrifice. Abraham replied: God will provide that. On the mountain Abraham built a stone altar and arranged the wood. Then he bound his son Isaac and laid him on the altar. He took the knife. At that moment he heard the voice: Abraham! Do not harm the boy! You have shown that

you are ready to obey me and trust in me. You were prepared to offer me your only son, Isaac.

When Abraham looked around he saw a ram which had become entangled in a thicket. He placed the animal on the altar and offered God the burnt offering. Then he came down the mountain with Isaac. (Gen 22)

9. Isaac, Esau and Jacob

Isaac inherited Abraham's herds, his servants and his maids. He also inherited God's blessing. Since his wife Rebecca was barren, Isaac prayed to God. God heard his prayer. Rebecca became a mother. She gave birth to two sons. They were twins, but from the moment of their birth they were completely different. The first-born had hair on his arms and legs. His parents called him Esau. The other son had a smooth skin. They called him Jacob. Esau grew up to be a hunter. Jacob was quiet and remained close to the tents, working as a shepherd and farmer. Isaac preferred Esau, for he liked to eat wild game; but Rebecca preferred Jacob.

Once, Jacob had just cooked some lentil soup, as Esau returned home exhausted from the hunt. Give me some of that red soup, he said. Jacob replied: First sell me your birthright. Esau replied: Here I am starving, what use is this right to me! He took an oath and sold Jacob his birthright. Only then did Jacob give him bread and lentil soup.

Isaac grew old. He could no longer see well. One day he said to Esau: Go out and hunt. Bring me wild game to eat. Then I will give you God's blessing. Rebecca heard what Isaac said. She wanted to secure the blessing for Jacob. So she said to him: Fetch two small kids. She roasted the goat meat. Then she covered his arms and neck with the goatskins and sent him to Isaac.

Isaac heard the footsteps. He asked: Who are you? I am Esau, said Jacob. I've brought you the roast meat. Eat first and then give me the blessing you promised. Isaac reached out for his son's arm. He felt the goat-skin, and it deceived him. He blessed Jacob: God give you everything that you need on earth. Blessed be he who blesses you!

Soon after, Esau returned from the hunt. He brought his father roast meat and asked him for the blessing. Then Isaac realised that his son Jacob had tricked him. But he could not take back the blessing that he had passed on to him. Esau grew angry. He said: When our father Isaac dies, I will kill Jacob. Rebecca heard this. She said to Jacob: Flee to your uncle Laban in Haran. You can wait there until Esau has forgotten his anger. Thus Jacob came to Laban. He worked as a shepherd for Laban. But he also tended his own flock. He married and had children.

After twenty years Jacob returned to Canaan with his whole family. He took his herds with him. Along the way he rested one night next to the river Jabbok.

He had sent all his belongings across to the other bank and had remained alone. That night someone wrestled with Jacob until daybreak. After the fight he blessed Jacob and said: From now on you will no longer be called Jacob, but Israel, which means: A fighter of God. For you have fought against God and men, and have prevailed.

Jacob made peace with his brother Esau. He lived in the land of Canaan and had twelve sons: Reuben, Simeon, Levi, Judah, Issachar, Zebulun, Joseph, Benjamin, Dan, Naphtali, Gad and Asher. They were the ancestors of the people of Israel. (Gen 25 - 35)

10. Joseph comes to Egypt

Jacob loved Joseph more than his other sons. He gave him a beautiful coat. The others became jealous. One day Jacob sent Joseph to his brothers who were out on the pastures. They grabbed him and threw him into an empty well. At first they wanted to kill their

brother, but then they sold him to foreign merchants
for twenty pieces of silver. The brothers tore up Joseph's coat and sprinkled it with lamb's blood. Then
they sent it to Jacob via a messenger. Jacob recognised the coat at once. He thought that a wild animal
had killed Joseph. For a long time Jacob mourned his
favourite son.

Joseph came to Egypt with the merchants. There
they sold him to the officer Potiphar. Joseph worked
for Potiphar, and all that he did turned out well. For
God was with him. Potiphar put Joseph in charge of
his household. Potiphar's wife tried to seduce Joseph.
Since Joseph refused, she lied about him to her husband. Thereupon Potiphar had Joseph thrown into
prison. At that time the Pharaoh's baker and his chief
cup-bearer were also in prison. They each had a dream. They described them to Joseph and he was able to
tell them what their dreams meant: The cup-bearer
would be released and would return to his work. The
baker would be condemned and executed. Everything
happened as Joseph had said. (Gen 37; 39 - 40)

11. Jacob and his sons come to Egypt

Two years later the Pharaoh, the King of Egypt, had a dream. He questioned all the wise men and dream interpreters in his land, but none of them was able to interpret his dream. Then the cup-bearer remembered Joseph. He said to Pharaoh: There is a young man in prison, an Israelite. He was able to interpret my dream and also the baker's. What he told us happened. The Pharaoh summoned Joseph. He described his dream: Seven healthy, fat cows come up out of the Nile. They are followed by seven lean and bony ones who devour them. Again, seven full, ripe ears of corn are growing on a single stalk. Then seven empty, withered ones come and thrust them aside. Joseph explained to the Pharaoh: During the night God has shown you what is to come: Seven good years, in which the cattle grow fat and the corn in the fields yields abundantly. They will be followed by seven bad years in which no rain falls. The animals will die of thirst, the corn will wither. I can give you this advice: Build warehouses and purchase the surplus in the good years. Build up a reserve for the years of famine. The Pharaoh trusted Joseph. He made him his administrator. After seven good harvests came the time when no rain fell, the cattle died of thirst and the crops withered. Then Joseph opened the warehouses. Hungry people came from far away to buy grain.

Jacob and his sons also had nothing more to eat. So Jacob sent his sons to Egypt. Joseph saw his brothers and recognised them immediately. But they did not recognise him. Joseph put his brothers to the test. He wanted to find out if they would stand up for one another. He ordered his silver cup to be placed in Benjamin's sack. As the brothers were on their way home, Joseph sent his steward after them. He halted them and accused them: Why have you repaid good with evil? Why have you stolen my master's silver cup? The brothers defended themselves: We have stolen nothing! But when Benjamin's sack was searched the cup was found.

The brothers returned together to Joseph. He said: You others can go! Only the one on whose person the cup was found must stay. Judah answered him: Our father loves his youngest son. He would die of grief if anything were to happen to him. Let me stay in Benjamin's place. Joseph could no longer contain himself: I am Joseph, your brother, he said. You sold me. You intended evil. But God has turned it to good. He allowed me to come to Egypt so that I could save you. Return quickly to our father and come with him to Egypt. Here you will suffer no want. Jacob rejoiced deeply when he heard that Joseph was alive. He and his sons and their families moved to Egypt. There they lived in the land of Goshen as shepherds. As long as the famine lasted, Joseph looked after his brothers. (Gen 41 - 47)

MOSES LEADS THE PEOPLE
THROUGH THE DESERT

12. God saves Moses

Joseph and his brothers died. Their children and grandchildren, the Israelites, lived in Egypt. There they became a great nation. Many years passed. A new Pharaoh ruled in Egypt. He knew nothing of Joseph or of how he had helped the Egyptians in a time of great famine. He was afraid of the Israelites and said: They are strong. Soon they will be stronger than we Egyptians. But I will stop them. First this Pharaoh had the Israelites do forced labour. They had to build cities. Then he commanded that all the first-born sons of the Israelites be drowned in the Nile river. When there are no more sons growing up, he thought, the nation will soon die out.

There was a mother who wanted to save her little son. First she hid him in the house, but then after three months she could hide him there no longer. So she wove a basket out of reeds and coated it with pitch, so that it was watertight. Then she put her little boy in the basket and hid him among the reeds on the Nile. Her daughter Miriam stayed on the bank to see what would happen to the basket.

Pharaoh's daughter came to the Nile. She wanted to bathe in the river. She noticed the basket and had her maid bring it to the shore. She saw the child and took pity on it. Then Miriam came out of hiding and asked: Should I look for a woman to nurse the small child for you? Yes, do that, said Pharaoh's daughter. So Miriam fetched her mother. Pharaoh's daughter gave the child to her to look after. She gave him the name of Moses.

When Moses was older he lived in the royal palace. He was brought up as if he were an Egyptian. But he never forgot that he belonged to the Israelite people, who were forced to do hard slave labour. Once he saw an Egyptian strike an Israelite. Moses was overcome with rage. He killed the Egyptian. So then he had to flee. He went into the land of Midian and worked as a shepherd in the house of the priest Jethro. (Ex 1 - 2)

13. God sends Moses

Moses was herding his flock in the wilderness. He came to Sinai, the mountain of God. There he saw a thornbush. It was burning and yet it was not being burned up. Filled with curiosity, Moses drew nearer. Then he heard a voice: Moses, Moses! I am the God of your father, the God of Abraham, Isaac and Jacob. Hearing this, Moses covered his face. He was afraid to look at God. But God spoke to him: I have seen how my people are maltreated in Egypt. I have heard their cries. I know their sufferings. And so I am sending you to Pharaoh. You are to lead my people out of

Egypt. Moses answered: Who am I to go to Pharaoh and give him orders? But God said: I shall be with you.

But Moses had another objection: The Israelites will not believe me if I tell them: The God of your fathers has sent me to you. They will ask me: Tell us his name. What answer shall I give them? God said: I AM who I AM. That is my name for all time. But Moses still did not want to obey God's command. He said: I am a poor speaker. Then God replied: Just go; I will tell you what to say. Please send someone else, protested Moses. But God had chosen Moses.

Moses returned with his family to Egypt. His brother Aaron came to meet him. Together they summoned all the fathers of the Israelite families? Moses told them what the God of Abraham, Isaac and Jacob had commanded him to do. The Israelites learned that God wanted to put an end to their distress. They put their trust in him and worshipped him. (Ex 3).

14. Set my people free!

Moses and Aaron went to Pharaoh. They demanded: Let our people go free! God wishes it. But Pharaoh had no intention of setting the Israelites free. He said: Who is the God of Israel that I should listen to him? I do not know him and I will not let the Israelites go. I will have them do even more work so that they do not forget who is their master. The same day he ordered the slave-drivers: Make the Israelites work so hard that they forget this idle talk.

The Israelites groaned under their burden. Moses implored the Lord, and God promised him: I am God and I will lead you out of Egypt. I will adopt you as my own people. You will recognize that I am your God. I will bring you to the land I promised Abraham, Isaac and Jacob. I will give it to you as your inheritance.

God let the Pharaoh feel his might. Terrible plagues struck Egypt. Hailstorms fell, crops were ruined, plagues contaminated the drinking water and killed cattle. Insects infested the houses. The air became so dirt-ridden that all the Egyptians broke out in sores and boils. The Pharaoh was quite aware of the source of this misfortune. Twice, three times he pretended he would free the Israelites from their slavery, but as soon as the plagues were over he broke his word. (Ex 5 - 11)

15. The first Passover

Then God said to Moses: Today, this very night, Pharaoh will let you go. Make yourselves ready to set out. Each family must slaughter a lamb. You must smear a sign on the doorposts with its blood. Put on sandals. Take a staff in your hand. Eat hastily and leave nothing over. This night all the first-born sons of the Egyptians will die. But the Angel of Death will pass over your houses, which have been marked by the blood of the lamb.

Everything happened just as God had said. The first-born sons of the Egyptians died. The son of the poorest man and also the Pharaoh's son. That night the Egyptians wept for their sons. Then the Pharaoh had Moses and Aaron brought to him and ordered them: Go away, quickly! Take everything that belongs to you. The Israelites gathered together and set off out of Egypt.

The people of Israel never forgot this first Passover night. The mothers and fathers did not forget how God had spared their own first-born sons. Since then they have always brought God an offering after the birth of their first son. Each year they celebrate the Passover, the feast of the Exodus, and they explain it to their children like this: With a mighty hand God liberated us from bondage in Egypt. (Ex 12 - 13)

16. God saves his people

Soon the Pharaoh regretted letting the Israelites go. He mustered his soldiers and charioteers and set out in pursuit of the Israelites. The Israelites had

pitched camp by the Red Sea. One of their guards saw the cloud of dust: The Egyptians are coming! The Israelites were terrified, for they were trapped. In front of them was the sea, behind them the heavily-armed enemy. They complained to Moses: Why did you lead us into the disaster? We will all perish here! But Moses said: Have no fear. Today you will witness God's power to save.

Moses stretched out his hand over the sea, as God had commanded. An east wind sprang up. It drove back the water. The people of Israel walked through the sea. Men and women, daughters and sons, cattle and sheep – a great procession. The Egyptians came to the shore. They did not hesitate for long and plunged after the Israelites. But the path the Israelites could take on account of their trust in God, became a path to death for the Egyptians. The water gushed back. Horses, chariots, the Pharaoh's entire army sank under the waves. The Israelites experienced how God saves. (Ex 14 - 15).

17. God cares for his people

From the Red Sea, Moses led the people of Israel through the desert. For three days they searched for water. Then at last they found a spring. But the water had a bitter taste. It was undrinkable. Then the Israelites rebelled against Moses: Now you are letting us die of thirst in the desert! Moses begged God: Help us! And God showed Moses a piece of wood. When Moses threw it into the spring the water turned sweet, and they could all quench their thirst.

Soon after they began to complain to Moses again: Why did you lead us into the desert? If only we had stayed in Egypt! There at least we had full pans of meat and all the bread we could eat! But God said to Moses: I will give you bread and meat, so that you learn that you can put your trust in me. And indeed, in the evening a great flock of birds flew around the Israelite's camp. The birds were easy to catch. And in the morning the ground was covered with sweet white grains of Manna. Everyone was able to gather it and they all had enough to eat. Not only that day, but every day. During the whole forty years that the people of Israel spent in the wilderness, God gave them bread and meat.

Since that time parents tell their children how God once cared for his people and how he still cares for them. All people should know that they can trust in him and rely on his help. (Ex 15,22 - 16,36)

18. God chooses a people

The people of Israel wandered through the desert from one stopping-place to another. During the third month they were camped on Mount Sinai. Moses climbed up the mountain to God. God commanded him: Say this to the people of Israel: You have seen that I am mightier than the Egyptians. I have carried you here on eagle's wings. If you listen to what I say and keep my Covenant, then you will become a people that is closer to me than all the other peoples. But you must belong to me like priests, who are ready to serve me. You are a chosen, holy people.

When Moses came down from the mountain and told the people what God had commanded, they all shouted with one voice: We are ready! We want to do all that God has said. We want to live as he wishes us to. On Sinai God gave his people commandments. They are for all people and for all time. All who are faithful to God will see that God is faithful to them. God said: I am the Lord your God. I brought you out of Egypt, out of the land of slavery.

1. You shall have no gods except me. You shall not make any images of God. You shall serve none except me.

2. You shall not utter God's name to misuse it.

3. Remember the seventh day and keep it holy. No one shall work on that day.

4. Honour your father and your mother.

5. You shall not murder.

6. You shall not commit adultery.

7. You shall not steal.

8. You shall not say anything untrue about your fellow man.

9. You shall not covet another man's wife.

10. You shall not covet another person's goods.

Moses carved the commandments that God had given his people onto two tablets of stone. He laid these tablets in the sacred Ark of the Covenant. They are the pledge of the Covenant which God has made with his people. (Ex 19 - 20)

19. Rules of life

Hear, O Israel: The Lord is your God - the Lord and no other. And so you must love him with all your heart and with all your soul and with all your strength. (Deut 6, 4-5)

When you besiege a town you must not cut down its fruit trees. You may eat the fruit from the trees but you must not cut them down. (Deut 20, 19)

Do not wrong the widow or the orphan. If you oppress them and they call out to me, I will come to their defence. (Ex 22, 22ff)

If you see someone else's ox or sheep straying, you must not stand idly by. You must lead it back to its owner. (Deut 22, 1)

If a poor man is working for you, you must not keep him waiting for his wages. Pay him his due on the very same day. (Deut 24, 14-15)

When you have taken your first harvest from your

27

olive-tree or from your vineyard, leave what remains on the trees and vines for the poor to gather. (Deut 24, 20-21)

Do not ill-treat the strangers who live in your land. Give them the same rights as you have yourselves. Love them as you love yourselves and do not forget that you were strangers in the land of Egypt. I the Lord your God tell you this. (Lev 19, 33-34)

Do not speak evil about the deaf man who cannot defend himself. Do not put obstacles in the way of the blind man, which might cause him to stumble. (Lev 19, 14)

Do not bear hatred for your brother in your heart. Reprimand your neighbour, otherwise you yourself will be guilty. Do not take revenge, and do not bear a grudge against anyone. Love your neighbour as yourself. (Lev 19, 17-18)

20. The death of Moses

God had freed his people from slavery in Egypt. For forty years in the wilderness the Israelites learnt

that they could trust God. They also learnt how people can live side-by-side with one another.

The men and women who had departed from Egypt with Moses all died in the desert. Moses, too, grew old. He knew that he was going to die. He therefore blessed the people. He said: How happy are you, O Israel! Who is like you, a people rescued by the Lord? Then he climbed up to the summit of Mount Nebo. There the Lord showed him the whole land of Canaan, that he had promised to his people. Moses died there on the frontier of the Promised Land. For God had told him: I will let you see the land, but you shall not cross into it. The Israelites mourned over Moses for thirty days. (Deut 33-34)

KINGS AND PROPHETS

21. In the Promised Land

Before his death Moses named Joshua as his successor. He was to lead the Israelites into the land of Canaan, in which Abraham, Isaac and Jacob had lived. However, the tribes which lived in Canaan did not want the Israelites to enter the land. Under Joshua's leadership the Israelites were faithful to God's promise. They did not let themselves be driven away. Gradually they conquered the land. They built villages there and lived as farmers, like the Canaanites.

The Israelites were able to learn a great deal from the Canaanites: when to sow the grain and harvest the grapes, how to make the best tools, how to cook and how to dress. But there was one thing they were not allowed to imitate from the Canaanites if they were to remain faithful to the Covenant with God - they must not worship the gods of the Canaanites, nor serve them. The Israelites found it hard to keep this commandment. For the Canaanites had places of sacrifice throughout the land, on mountains and under tall trees, and they worshipped their gods there, praying for rain and a good harvest.

The Israelites discovered something new during this time: as long as they were faithful to the God of Abraham, Isaac and Jacob, he would give them blessing and protection. But when they were unfaithful they experienced suffering and hardship. However, when they returned to him, admitted their guilt and begged his forgiveness, then he would turn back to them once more and bless them. (Jos; Jg)

22. The people want a king

The Israelites divided up the land in such a way that each of the twelve great tribes received a territory of its own. The elders of the tribes shared out the land among the families. Each family received enough to satisfy all its needs.

Each of the tribes lived independently. But when they were threatened by an enemy they defended themselves together. And God would grant them a saviour, who would lead them out of danger.

But then Israel began to find it very hard to trust in God alone and to wait for him to send them a saviour every time they were in need. They wanted a permanent leader - a king. Samuel was a judge sent by God. He asked them: Do you really wish to bow down before a man, to work for him, pay him taxes? But the representatives of the tribes said: We want to be like the other nations. A king should tell us what is right and what is wrong. A king should lead us in battle.

God spoke to Samuel: Listen to what the men are demanding. It is not you that they have rejected, but me. Then Samuel anointed Saul in the name of God as King of Israel. God bestowed his Spirit upon him. Saul might have remained a good king if he himself had trusted God with all his heart. But Saul did not want to rely on another person - not even on God. He did not trust anyone. He became sad and confused. God was no longer with Saul. So Saul was unable to lead the people of Israel or to defend them any more. (1 Sam 8 - 15)

23. David, the shepherd from Bethlehem

David of Bethlehem became the second and the greatest king of Israel. He trusted God and God was with him. And so the people of God cannot forget the name of David. In Israel many stories are told about him.

David was the youngest son of Jesse. He was guarding the sheep when Samuel came to anoint him king. David was a good shepherd. He knew his sheep and loved them and did not run away when a wild animal came prowling round. David was brave. He had no fear of the enemies of God and his people. When he was still a youth, he went to visit his brothers in the battle-camp. There he saw how a huge and powerful man, the giant Goliath, was mocking the Israelites and

their God. None of the Israelites dared to do battle with Goliath. But David said to him: You will find out how strong the God of Israel is. David placed a stone in his sling, whirled it around above his head and let it fly. It struck the giant Goliath in the middle of his forehead. At that the enemy took fright. They no longer wanted to fight against Israel. They ran away.

David could sing and play the harp. In the Book of Psalms, the hymn-book of the people of God, there are one hundred and fifty songs that David used to sing. For a time David lived in King Saul's palace. Whenever Saul was sad, David would play on the harp. Then Saul would become happy again. David was able to defeat all their enemies, because God was with him. So Saul made him the commander of his army. But because David won so many victories and was so popular with the people, Saul became jealous. He wanted to get rid of David. For many years David and a group of his friends had to hide from Saul.

When the Philistines went to war against Israel once more, Saul's army was unable to stand up against them. Saul's three sons died in the mountains of Gilboa. Saul himself was seriously wounded. Then he threw himself upon his own sword. (1 Sam 16-31)

24. David, king in Jerusalem

After Saul's death, David became king over all of Israel. He conquered Jerusalem and made it into the capital city. He had the Holy Ark of the Covenant brought to Jerusalem, together with the tablets of stone on which the commandments of the covenant were written. He wanted Jerusalem to be the city of God.

David trusted God. He wanted to stay faithful to the Covenant. When he had done something evil he admitted his guilt and asked God to forgive him. One day David summoned Nathan. Nathan was a man whom God had chosen as his spokesman - a prophet.

David said to Nathan: I am living in a splendid palace, but the Holy Ark is still in a tent. I want to build a house for God.

The next day Nathan came back to David and said: God does not want you to build him a house. On the contrary, he will build you a house - a living house. When you die, your son will rule over God's people. This word holds true for ever. And so the people of God believe that the great Saviour, the Messiah whom God had promised to man, will come from the family of David. (2 Sam 7)

25. One of David's songs

Lord, you are my Shepherd,
and so I lack nothing.
You lead me to green pastures
and to a resting-place beside the water.
You show me paths that are safe.
Even when I have to walk
through the dark valley
I am not afraid
because you are at my side. (Ps 23)

26. Solomon builds God a house

King David died and was buried in Jerusalem. His son Solomon ruled over Israel.

Solomon was a wise king. He knew what was right and what was wrong. In Jerusalem he built himself a palace, and he also built a house for God - the temple. There he brought the Ark of the Covenant. On the day when the temple was consecrated Solomon prayed: O Lord, my God! You have promised that you will be near to us in this temple. Hear my prayer. Hear all those who call upon you in this house. Hear us and forgive us our guilt!

Solomon did not need to wage any wars as his father David had done. He made treaties with other nations. He engaged in trade and sent out ships across the sea. He brought foreign workers into his country and married foreign women. The foreigners whom Solomon had brought into the country wanted to worship their own gods. Solomon allowed them to build altars for their gods in the land of Israel. Solomon even prayed to the gods of the foreigners and worshipped them. Thus he betrayed the one God. He broke the Covenant. (1 Kings 5 - 11)

27. Solomon's proverbs

A willing son is his father's joy; a stubborn son his mother's grief. (10,1)

Hatred stirs up strife; but love creates harmony. (10,12)

Whoever helps others, will himself be helped; whoever gives water to the thirsty, will not thirst himself. (11,25)

Whoever keeps to honest ways, respects God; he whose ways are crooked, scorns him. (14,2)

Whoever despises his neighbour, sins; whoever takes pity on the poor is blessed. (14,21)

Whoever closes his ear to the cry of the poor, will not be heard when he cries out for help himself. (21,13)

28. Two kings in one nation

After Solomon's death, his son Rehoboam wanted to be king in Jerusalem. Wise men gave him this advice: Your father exacted many tributes from the farmers and heavy taxes from the merchants. If you demand less, all of Israel will acknowledge you as king.

But Rehoboam did not listen to the advice of the wise men. And so the ten tribes who lived in the north of the country said: We do not need a king from David's house. We will choose our own king. Only the tribe of Judah, which was named after the son of Jacob and lived near to Jerusalem, remained true to Rehoboam. From then on there was not only a king ruling in Jerusalem, but also one in Sichem, or Samaria. (1 Kings 12)

29. The Living God

Jeroboam, the first king of the northern tribes, said to himself: It is not good that the people of my kingdom have to go to the temple in Jerusalem when they wish to hold a religious ceremony or offer up a sacrifice. And so he had two golden calves made. One he erected in the north of his kingdom, in the city of Dan, and the other in the south, in the city of Bethel. Then he announced to all the people: You no longer need to go up to Jerusalem when you want to celebrate a feast or offer up a sacrifice. You will find God in Dan and in Bethel - the same God who brought your fathers out of the land of Egypt.

Not all the Israelites listened to Jeroboam, for they remembered that God had forbidden them to make images of God as the Egyptians had done. They knew they would break the Covenant if they exchanged the living God for a lifeless idol. (1 Kings 12; Ex 32 - 34)

30. The Mighty God

Often the kings of Israel forgot God and his Covenant. But God kept the Covenant. He sent the kings and the people men who spoke in his Name - the prophets.

King Ahab was one of those who worshipped the god Baal. Elijah was a prophet of God. He went to King Ahab and said: I serve the God of Israel. He is the mighty God. You will see his might, and the whole land along with you, for from today no more dew will fall from the heavens, and no rain either. The drought will last as long as I command it to.

Elijah feared the anger of the king. He fled across the border to Phoenicia. There he lived in the house of a poor woman. She was a widow and had an only son. Her son fell ill and died. Then the woman complained to Elijah: You are a man of God. You live in my house. So God looks at me. He sees my sins and punishes me. Elijah lifted up the dead child and laid him on his own bed. Then he bent over the young boy and prayed: Lord, my God, give this child back his life. God heard the prayer of his prophet. The child came back to life. Elijah took the boy by the hand and brought him to his mother. (1 Kings 17)

31. The One True God

After two years God sent Elijah to King Ahab once more. Ahab accused the prophet: Because of you the whole people of Israel have nothing to eat! But Elijah answered him: Not I, but you and your family are to blame for the prolonged drought. You have deserted our God and gone running after Baal. Now summon

all the people to Mount Carmel. There it will be decided who is the one true God. King Ahab called everyone together. Not only the prophets and priests came to Mount Carmel but also many Israelites.

Elijah said: Build an altar and put the beast of sacrifice on it. Then pray to your god. Perhaps he will send down fire from heaven and accept your sacrifice. The priests and prophets of Baal built the altar and put the sacrifice on it. From early morning till midday they prayed. From midday until evening they cried out: Baal, hear us! But they called out in vain. Nothing happened.

In the evening Elijah built an altar for the God of Israel. He put the sacrifice on the altar and poured water over it. Then he prayed: Lord, you are the God of Abraham, the God of Isaac and the God of Jacob. Show everyone that you are the God of Israel and that I am your servant. Hear me, O Lord! Hear me! Then fire fell from Heaven. The sacrifice was burnt up. All those who saw it were afraid. They cried out: The Lord is God! The Lord is God! Soon after clouds appeared. Rain began to fall on the parched land. (1 Kings 18)

32. God calls Elijah to him

Elijah was aware that God wished to call him to himself. He went into the region beyond the Jordan. He wanted to be alone. But Elisha, his pupil, did not want to leave him alone. He went with Elijah. Elisha saw how fire came down from heaven, a mighty whirlwind. It surrounded Elijah and carried him up to heaven as if in a chariot.

As Elisha came back across the Jordan alone, he met fifty disciples of the prophet. They asked: Where is Elijah? Let us look for him! You will not find him, answered Elisha. For three days they searched for Elijah but did not find him. They came back and said: God has taken the prophet to himself in a fiery chariot. Since then the people of Israel believe that at the end of time God will send his messenger Elijah back to earth again. (2 Kings 2)

33. The hungry are fed

A man came to the prophet Elisha and brought him twenty barley loaves and a sack of grain. Elisha said to his servant: Share them out so that all may eat. The servant answered: How can a hundred men be fed with that? But Elisha repeated his words: Give them to the people to eat. You will see that there will be left-overs. The servant shared out the food. When everyone had eaten, left-overs remained. It was just as the Lord had said through Elisha. (2 Kings 4, 42ff)

34. God's sign for his people

While Ahaz was king in Jerusalem, two kings declared war on him. They surrounded Jerusalem with their soldiers. The King's heart and the hearts of the people trembled, just like trees in the forest tremble when the storm breaks out upon them.

King Ahaz went to the water channel to inspect it.

The prophet Isaiah went there also. He brought the king a message from God: Stay calm, do not fear. The two are plotting evil against you. Be loyal to God and he will be loyal to you. Isaiah said: God will give you a sign - any sign you ask for - so that you can be sure of his help. But Ahaz rejected the offer: No, I will not ask God for a sign: Then Isaiah said: Nevertheless, God will give you this sign: See, the maiden shall conceive a child. She will give birth to a son and give him the name Immanuel. That means: God is with us. (Is 7)

35. The Prophet Amos accuses

The Lord says this: For the three crimes, the four crimes of Judah, I will not take back my punishment. They have despised my word and disobeyed my commandments. They have let false gods lead them astray, just like their ancestors. And so I am going to hurl fire on Judah, and burn up the palaces of Jerusalem.

The Lord says this: For the three crimes, the four crimes of Israel, I will not hold back my punishment. They have sold the innocent man for money. They have trampled the little ones into the dust and cheated the weak out of their rights.

And so I will let the earth shudder beneath you just as a harvest-waggon sways under the weight of the sheaves. Even the quickest cannot escape, the strength of the strongest fails them, the bravest lose courage. (Amos 2)

36. Jeremiah warns of God's punishment

The people who lived in a Covenant with God were not numerous. Their troops were no match for the armies of the mighty nations. They could not prevent the Assyrians from occupying the land and driving many people out of their own country and into foreign lands. Those who were believers recognised God's punishment in this misfortune, just as he had warned through his prophets.

In Jerusalem, Jeremiah warned the people: For twenty-three years now I have been God's prophet. I have passed on to you all that he has said. But you will not listen. I said: Be converted from your wrongful ways. Stop doing evil. Then you will remain in the land which God has given to your fathers and you for ever. But you have not listened to me. And so the Lord has said: I will allow the nations of the North to invade. I will make Nebuchadnezzar, the King of Babylon, into my instrument. I will make him fall upon you and your neighbours. He will devastate your land. You will serve the King of Babylon.

And so it happened: Nebuchadnezzar laid siege to Jerusalem with his army. Soon there was no more bread to be had in the city. The famine became extreme. Then the Babylonians made a breach in the wall. They forced their way into the city, burned down the temple, the king's palace and the big houses. The walls of Jerusalem were torn down. The sacred vessels of the temple were taken as booty by the Babylonians. All the important people, and the craftsmen too, were forced into exile in Babylon. Only the poor people, the peasants and the vine-growers were allowed to stay behind in their homeland. (Jer 25 ; 52)

37. God wishes to forgive his people

God spoke to his people through his prophet Ezekiel: Because you were unfaithful to me, because you did not listen to my word but violated my commandments - you have lost your country and must now live in exile. But the Babylonians are now saying: This is God's people, surely? Why have they lost their land? They are mocking you, and mocking me. But they will learn that I am the Lord. I will gather you together and lead you back into your own land. I will make you into new men - men who will serve me faithfully. I will take out the heart of stone from your bodies and give you a human heart. I will bestow my Spirit upon you so that you respect my commandments and fulfil them. You will live in the land which I gave to your ancestors. You will be my people and I will be your God. (Ezek 36, 20-28)

38. Return from Babylon

The exiled people from Judah and Jerusalem had to remain about forty years in Babylon. Then Cyrus, the Persian king, conquered Babylon. He proclaimed throughout his kingdom: The Lord, the God of heaven, has given me power over all the kingdoms of the earth. He has ordered me to rebuild his house in Jerusalem. Everyone who belongs to God's people shall return to Jerusalem. And there they should rebuild the temple.

And so they set out - all who were moved by God's Spirit. Their neighbours gave them gold and silver, cattle and other gifts. King Cyrus had the sacred ves-

sels fetched, which Nebuchadnezzar had looted from the temple and taken to Babylon. (Ezra 1)

39. A Song of Homecoming

When the Lord ended our captivity and brought us home to Jerusalem, it seemed like a dream for us. Our mouth was filled with laughter, we could only shout for joy.

Then the other nations said: The Lord has done great things for them! Yes, the Lord has done great things for us, we are overjoyed. (Ps 126)

WAITING FOR THE MESSIAH

40. The Jewish people

The families that returned from exile in Babylon had their homes in the land of the tribe of Judah, in and around Jerusalem. They became the core of the Jewish people. They wanted to live as their fathers had done. But nothing was the same any more. The Babylonians had brought foreign settlers into Jerusalem and its surroundings. They lived according to their own customs and served their own gods.

The walls which had protected Jerusalem had been torn down. The temple which Solomon had built was a heap of rubble. The Jews rebuilt their houses and the walls around Jerusalem. In the second year after their homecoming they laid the foundation-stone for the second temple.

The Jews were living once more in their own land. But this land was now part of the great realms of foreign kings. They sent their soldiers, their tax-collectors and their governors to Jerusalem. There were times when these foreigners tried to turn the Jews away from the faith of Abraham; times when a foreign king would try to force all those who belonged to his kingdom to live and believe according to his ways and to serve his gods.

During these centuries the priests in Jerusalem gathered together all the sacred writings and traditions. All this time the devout people adhered to all the laws and instructions. They gained a new understanding of God and his Covenant. They hoped for the King, the Redeemer, whom God had promised to his people. They were persecuted and tortured. But even as they faced death they declared their faith in the living God, who can rescue his own people through death from death. (Ezra; Neh; Macc)

41. Job demands an answer from God

Job was a devout man. He trusted God and despised evil. Job was a wealthy man. He had seven sons, three daughters, and many sheep as well as camels, oxen and she-asses. For Job it was not hard to be faithful to God, who had given him all these things.

But God put Job to the test. Bands of robbers fell upon his herds. They killed the shepherds and stole the beasts. Yet Job was not disconcerted. He trusted God. Soon, a second disaster befell him. As his sons and daughters were sitting together at table a whirlwind came and destroyed the house. Job's sons and daughters were killed by the falling rubble. When Job heard of the tragedy he said: I was naked when I came into the world. I will be naked when I die. The Lord gives and he takes. I praise him.

But still worse sufferings befell Job. He became a leper. His whole body was covered with sores. The rich man, Job, sat upon a heap of ashes. He scratched himself with a piece of broken pottery. Job's wife came to her husband and said: See what your faith in God has done for you! Curse God and die. But Job replied: You are talking like someone who does not know God. If we accept the good things that he sends, must we not also accept the bad things from his hand?

Job had three friends. When they heard of his misfortune they came to see him. They wanted to comfort him. But when they saw him in all his misery, they began to weep. They sat next to him - for seven days and seven nights. None of them said a single word, for they could see how great Job's suffering was. Then Job began to talk with God and to dispute with him. He complained of his suffering and he complained to God for having sent him - an innocent man - so much misfortune.

Job's friends were horrified. They wanted to defend God and said: How can you accuse God? Everyone knows that he is just. He rewards good and he punishes evil. He would not have sent you this suffering if you had not deserved such punishment. But Job was quite sure of his cause. He demanded that God should explain to him how he, a devout man, had come to deserve such suffering.

His friends held long speeches to convince Job that he must be wrong, because God could not be unjust. But Job would not give up. He wanted to understand why God was rewarding faithfulness with evil. Then God spoke to Job out of the whirlwind. He asked: Who are you to call me to account? Why do you speak of things which you cannot understand? Where were you when I laid the foundations of the earth? Did you divide the land from the sea? Did you give the day and the night their appointed times? Do you let the stars rise in the sky? Do you provide food for the animals of the earth? Job heard the questions, but he had no answer. And he realised that God is great beyond all understanding. So great that he can be trusted, even when his plans are not understood.

Job answered the Lord: Now I know that you can do all things. Whatever you plan, you can accomplish. Out of ignorance I demanded that you account for yourself. Your plans are wonderful. I cannot comprehend them. Until now I have only known you from hearsay. But now I have seen you with my own eyes.

And so I take back all that I have said and put my trust in you. (Job)

42. Jonah comes to know God

God spoke to his prophet Jonah: Set out on a journey. Go to Nineveh, the capital of the Assyrian kingdom, and tell all who live there that my chastisement will fall upon them. But Jonah did not want to go to Nineveh. He ran away and boarded a ship bound for a distant land. He wanted to get far away from God.

But the Lord sent a great storm at sea. It shook the ship from stem to stern. Everyone was afraid. Everyone prayed to his own god. But Jonah was sleeping below decks. The captain woke Jonah: How can you go on sleeping? Get up! Pray to your God! Perhaps he will save us. The sailors said: Let us cast lots to find out who is to blame for this disaster. The lot fell upon Jonah. Jonah said: Throw me into the sea; then you will be saved. It is my fault that this storm has come upon you. The sailors rowed with all their might. But they saw that they were getting nowhere against the storm. Then they prayed: Lord, do not hold what we are about to do as an offence against an innocent man. Then they took hold of Jonah and threw him into the sea. At once the sea grew calm.

But the Lord sent a great fish. It swallowed Jonah. For three days and three nights Jonah was in the belly of the fish. There he prayed to the Lord, his God. The fish swam to the shore and spat Jonah out. Once more, God ordered Jonah: Go to Niniveh, into the great city. Proclaim there everything that I will tell you. Jonah went to Niniveh. He announced: Only forty days more and Niniveh will be destroyed!

The people of Niniveh listened to Jonah. They believed God. They began a great fast and put on sackcloth by way of repentance. All of them: high and low, rich and poor, the entire population. God saw the repentance of the people of Niniveh. He withdrew his threat. But Jonah was unhappy and indignant. He prayed: Ah, Lord, I did not want to go to Niniveh. For I knew that you love people and forgive them. I would rather be dead than live through that!

Jonah left Niniveh and headed east. He sat down and waited to see what would happen. God caused a castor-oil plant to spring up and shelter Jonah with its shade. Jonah was delighted with the plant. But in the night a worm gnawed through its roots and the plant withered. The sun was scorching. Jonah could not bear the heat. He said: I wish I were dead. But God asked Jonah: You are upset about a castor-oil plant that sprang up in a night and withered in a night. And am I not to feel sorry for the great city of Niniveh, with its many children and many animals? (Jonah)

43. God's reign

The prophet Daniel describes the vision which God granted him: Thrones were set up. One of great age took his seat. His robe was white as snow, his hair

as white as pure wool, his throne a blaze of flames and
its wheels of glowing fire. A stream of fire emanated
from him. A thousand thousand served him. Ten thousand times ten thousand stood before him.

And see, on the clouds of heaven there came One
like a Son of Man. He came to the One of great age and
was led into his presence. The One of great age gave
him power, glory and sovereignty. All peoples, men of
all languages and races served him. His rule is an
eternal rule which will never pass away. His kingdom
is indestructible. (Dan 7, 9-14)

44. A song about the Servant of God

A prophet sings songs about the servant who does
God's will in all things. Through him, the obedient
one, God's justice and salvation descend upon the
earth:

See, this is my servant; I support him. He is my
chosen one; I love him. I have given him my Spirit. He

proclaims the truth to the nations. He does not yell, he does not shout, he does not make his voice heard in the streets. He does not break the crushed reed nor snuff out the dimly burning wick. In fidelity he brings about justice. He does not tire, he does not break down until he has established my justice on earth. The farthest islands wait for his instruction. (Is 42, 1-4)

45. God's new world

The Lord says: I make all things new; a new heaven and a new earth. What once was, will be forgotten. You will be glad and will rejoice at what I am creating. There will be no more tears and no more sorrow. There will be no more children living only a few days. No men and women dying in the prime of life. They will live as long as trees. No one will take from them what their hands have made. Even before they call I shall answer them. Then the wolf and the lamb will feed side by side. The lion will eat straw like the ox. No one will do evil, no one will do harm. (Is 65, 17-25)

FROM THE BOOKS
OF THE NEW TESTAMENT

GOD KEEPS HIS WORD:
JESUS IS THE MESSIAH

46. He is the Son of the Most High

God sent the angel Gabriel as his messenger to Nazareth, to a virgin called Mary. She was engaged to Joseph, a man from the family of King David. Gabriel came to Mary and said: Rejoice, Mary! God is with you. He has chosen you. Mary was afraid and wondered what these words could mean. But Gabriel said: Do not be afraid Mary, for you have found favour with God. God loves you. You will conceive a child; you will bear a son. You are to give him the name Jesus. He will be great and will be called Son of the Most High.

Mary asked: How is this to happen, since I know no man? Gabriel answered her: The Holy Spirit, the power of the Most High will come over you. For nothing is impossible to God. Then Mary said: I am the handmaid of the Lord. May what God wills happen to me. (Lk 1, 27-38)

47. His name is Immanuel - 'God is with us'

Joseph was a just and pious man. He noticed that Mary, to whom he was betrothed, was expecting a child. Since he loved her and did not want to do her an injustice, he thought about how he could separate himself from her without attracting attention. That night, however, he saw a messenger from God, an angel. The angel said to him: Joseph, son of David, do not be afraid. Take Mary as your wife. The child she is expecting comes from God's Spirit. She will have a son and you shall call him Jesus. For he will reconcile the people with God. Thus the words spoken by the prophet Isaiah were fulfilled: Behold, the virgin will conceive. She will give birth to a son who will be called Immanuel. His name means: 'God is with us'. (Mt 1)

48. He is born in Bethlehem

At that time the Emperor Augustus ruled in Rome. He issued the order: All men living in my empire shall register their names on a list; each in the place from which his family comes. So Joseph took Mary and set out from Nazareth to Bethlehem, the home city of the family of David. There Mary gave birth to a son, her first-born. She wrapped him in swaddling clothes and laid him in a manger, because there was no room at the inn.

Near Bethlehem there were shepherds, guarding their sheep. God's messenger came to them. They were bathed in his shining brightness. The shepherds were very afraid. But the angel said: Do not fear. I bring you and the whole people a great joy: Today in the city of David the Saviour has been born; he is the Lord. You will recognise him thus: a child, wrapped in swaddling clothes, lying in a manger.

Suddenly there was a vast throng of angels on the field. They praised God and cried out: In heaven jubilant songs are sung to God and on earth men have peace because God loves them. Then the shepherds were alone again. They said to one another: Come, let us go to Bethlehem and see what has happened there. They hurried there and found Mary and Joseph, and the child lying in the manger. They saw for themselves and passed on to others what God had told them about this child. Everyone who heard them was

astonished. Mary, however, kept all these things in her heart and pondered on them.

The shepherds returned to their flocks. They sang hymns of praise and thanked God for everything they had heard and seen. When the child was eight days old he was given the name that Gabriel had announced: Jesus - meaning, 'God saves'. (Lk 2, 1-21)

49. He is the King of the Jews

At the time that Jesus was born, Herod ruled in Jerusalem as king. Then wise men from the East came to Jerusalem. They asked: Where is the new-born King of the Jews? We have seen how his star has risen. Now we have come to pay homage to him.

When King Herod heard this he was terrified. The inhabitants of Jerusalem shared his anxiety. Herod summoned the priests and the teachers who knew the Holy Books. he asked them: Where will the Messiah, the Saviour be born? They replied: he will be born in Bethlehem. That is what the prophet Micah has said: You, Bethlehem, in the land of Judah, are an important city of princes; for in you will be born the one who is to lead and guide the people of Israel.

Herod sent the wise men to Bethlehem: Go, look for the child! When you have found him, let me know, so that I also may go and worship him. As the wise men set off on their journey, the star they had seen in the East went ahead of them. It stopped over the house where Jesus was. They rejoiced from the bottom of their hearts. They entered the house, found Mary and the child, bowed down deeply and worshipped him. Then they gave him their gifts : gold, frankincense and myrrh. In the night, however, God told them not to return to Herod. So they left for their homeland by another route. (Mt 2, 1-12)

50. He is hunted

In the night God commanded Joseph in a dream:
Arise! Take the child and his mother. Go to Egypt and
remain there, until I tell you otherwise. Herod wants
to find the child and kill him. Straightaway in the
night, Joseph got up and fled to Egypt with Mary and
the child Jesus. But Herod noticed that the wise men
did not come back to Jerusalem. He was furious and
ordered that all boys in Bethlehem and in the immed-
iate vicinity of the city, who were younger than two
years old, should be killed. Later, after Herod had
died, an angel told Joseph in a dream: Arise! Take the
child and his mother. Go back to the land of Israel.
Joseph got up. He returned to the land of Israel with
Mary and the child Jesus. There they settled in Nazareth. (Mt 2, 13-23)

51. He belongs to God

Every year Jesus' parents went on a pilgrimage to
Jerusalem for the Feast of the Passover. When Jesus

was twelve years old they took him with them. After the feast days were over they set off home. Jesus, however, remained in Jerusalem. His parents did not notice this. That evening they looked for him among their relatives and friends. When they did not find him, they made their way back to Jerusalem. They searched for their son throughout the city. On the third day they found him in the temple. Jesus was sitting with the teachers of the Holy Scriptures. He was listening to them and asking questions. Everyone was amazed at his intelligent questions and answers.

When his parents saw him, they were overcome. His mother said to him: my child, why have you done this? Your father and I have been searching for you, full of apprehension. Jesus replied: Why were you looking for me? Did you not know that I belong in my Father's house? Then Jesus returned with them to Nazareth and was obedient to them. (Lk 2, 41-52)

52. The witness of John the Baptist

John, the son of the priest Zachariah and his wife Elizabeth, lived in the desert. When God called him to be his messenger, he went to a place near the Jordan river and said to the people: Mend your ways! Change your lives! Be baptised in the Jordan so that God will forgive your guilt. It was as the prophet Isaiah had written:

A voice cries in the wilderness: Prepare a way for the Lord, make a straight path for God. Every valley shall be raised, every mountain and hill shall be levelled. What is crooked shall be made straight and what is rough, smooth. And all mankind shall see God's gift of salvation. (Is 40, 3-5)

Many people came to John at the Jordan. They requested baptism and asked: What should we do? John said: Whoever has two cloaks should give one to someone who has none. Whoever has enough to eat should share with the hungry. To the tax-collectors he said: Do not demand more than is stipulated. And to the soldiers: Do not plunder, do not blackmail, and be content with your pay. Many thought that John was the Messiah, the Saviour. But John said to them: I am baptising you only with water. After me there will come One who is mightier than I. I am not worthy to undo his sandal straps. He will baptise you with the Holy Spirit and with the fire of judgement. (Lk 3, 1-18)

53. The testimony of the Father

When Jesus was about thirty years old, he came to John at the Jordan. He let himself be baptised like the others. Then he prayed. At that moment heaven opened and the Holy Spirit descended upon Jesus like a hovering dove. A voice spoke from heaven: You are my beloved son. My favour rests on you. (Lk 3, 21-23)

JESUS TEACHES AND HEALS: CHANGE YOUR LIFE

54. The Message of Jesus

Jesus came to Galilee. He preached the Gospel of God and said: The time has come. The Kingdom of God is at hand. Mend your ways and believe in the message that I bring. (Mk 1, 14-15)

When Jesus came to his home town of Nazareth, he went to the synagogue on the Sabbath. There he read out a passage from the book of the prophet Isaiah: The Spirit of God, the Lord, is upon me because he has chosen me. He has sent me to preach the Good News to the poor; to say to prisoners: you are free; and to the blind: you shall see; to the oppressed: you are liberated; and to proclaim the time of God's mercy.

Jesus explained to those who were in the synagogue: The words that you have just heard have been fulfilled today. At first they were all thrilled. But then they began to think: Is he not the son of Joseph? Jesus replied: Amen, I say to you, no prophet is accepted in his own country.

When the people in the synagogue heard this they were filled with rage. They jumped up and forced Jesus out of the city, intending to throw him down a cliff. But they were unable to do Jesus any harm. (Lk 4, 16-30)

55. Fishermen decide to follow Jesus

Jesus came to the shore of the sea of Galilee. There he saw Simon, also called Peter, and his brother Andrew. They were about to cast out their nets, for they were fishermen. Jesus said to them: Come with me. I will make you fishers of men. They both dropped their nets immediately and followed Jesus.

Shortly afterwards Jesus saw James, the son of Zebedee, and his brother John. They were in a boat with their father, mending their nets. Jesus called them. At once they left the boat and their father, and followed him. (Mt 4, 18-22)

56. A paralytic walks

Jesus came to Capernaum again. Soon the whole town knew that he was there. The people came running and crowded into the house and round the doors. Jesus told them all that God loves them.

Then four men came, carrying a paralysed man. They wanted to bring their friend to Jesus, but the crowd did not move aside. They could not get through. So the four men climbed onto the flat roof. They made a hole in the ceiling, just above the place where Jesus was. Then they lowered the paralysed man on the stretcher. Jesus saw that these men trusted him. He said to the paralytic: Your guilt is forgiven.

Some scribes heard what Jesus said. They thought: How dare he speak like that? That is blasphemy! No man can forgive sins. Only God has the power to do that. Jesus read their thoughts. He said to them: What are these thoughts in your hearts? Which is easier to say: Your sins are forgiven, or: Lame man, get up, take your stretcher and walk? But you are to see that I can forgive sins on earth by the authority of the Father. And he said to the paralytic: Get up! Take your stretcher and go home! The man stood up immediately, took his stretcher and left. Everyone could see it. They praised God and said to one another: We have never seen anything like this. (Mk 2, 1-12)

57. Jesus calls a sinner

Tax-collectors did not have a good reputation. They often demanded higher taxes than were actually prescribed. They worked for the Romans, who were occupying the country. For this reason the Pharisees did not want to have anything to do with them.

One day Jesus was walking along the shore of the sea of Galilee when he saw the tax-collector, Levi, sitting in his booth. Jesus said to him: Come, follow me. Levi got up and went with Jesus. When Jesus was dining in Levi's house, many tax-collectors and sinners also ate with him and his disciples. The Pharisees and scribes saw this and said to his disciples: How can he dine in the company of sinners? Jesus heard the question and replied: It is not the healthy, but the sick who need the doctor. I have not come to call the just, but sinners. (Mk 2, 13-17)

58. Jesus chooses the twelve Apostles

Jesus went up a mountain. He summoned the disciples he had chosen and they came over to him; twelve men. They were to accompany him always; to see what he did and hear what he taught. He wanted to send these twelve out as his apostles, so that they might pass on the Good News and heal the sick in his name. The twelve were: Simon, to whom he gave the name Peter, James and his brother John, then Andrew, Philip, Bartholomew, Matthew (also called Levi), Thomas, James the son of Alpheus, Thaddaeus, Simon and Judas Iscariot, who later betrayed him. (Mk 3, 13-19)

59. Jesus chooses a people

Jesus wandered through Galilee. He taught in the synagogues and proclaimed the Gospel of God. He healed all those who were sick and suffering. Throughout the country people were talking about him. Men came to him from far and wide. Seeing that a large crowd had gathered, Jesus went up a hill. He sat down and his disciples joined him. He began to teach:

All those who know they are poor in the eyes of God can rejoice, for the kingdom of heaven belongs to them.

All those who are in sorrow can rejoice; for God will give them possession of the earth.

All those who do not resort to violence can rejoice; for God will give them possession of the earth.

All those who yearn that God's will be done can rejoice; for God will fulfil their longing.

All those who are merciful can rejoice; for God will have mercy on them.

All those who have a pure heart can rejoice; for they will see God.

All those who create peace can rejoice; for God will make them his children.

All those who are persecuted because they do

God's will can rejoice; for the kingdom of heaven belongs to them (Mt 4, 23-25; 5, 1-10).

60. Jesus' Rules of Life

You know the commandment that states: do not murder. Whoever kills another is liable to judgement. Now I tell you: Whoever is angry at his brother is liable to judgement. (Mt 5, 21)

If you are on your way to bring a gift to God and you remember that your brother has something against you, leave your gift before the altar. Turn around, be reconciled with your brother. Then come and offer your gift. (Mt 5, 23)

You know the commandment that states: Married people must be faithful to one another. Now I tell you: whoever covets another woman or another man in their heart, has been unfaithful. (Mt 5, 27-28)

You have learned: Love your neighbour and hate your enemy. Now I tell you: Love your enemies and do good to those who act against you. When you do that you are children of your Father in heaven. He lets the sun shine on good and bad alike. He sends rain on the just and the unjust. (Mt 5, 43-45)

Love your enemies, help them and lend them what they lack, even when you cannot count on having it returned. God will reward you: you will be his children. For he is good even towards the ungrateful and sinners. Be merciful, just as he is. (Lk 6, 35-36)

Do not judge one another, and God will not judge you. Do not condemn anyone, and God will not condemn you. Forgive one another's debt, and God will forgive you. Give, and God will give to you. (Lk 6, 37-38)

61. A prayer for the disciples

Jesus said to his disciples: This is how you must pray:

Our Father, who art in heaven, hallowed be thy name; thy kingdom come; thy will be done on earth, as it is in heaven. Give us this day our daily bread; and forgive us our trespasses as we forgive those who trespass against us; and lead us not into temptation, but deliver us from evil. (Mt 6, 9-13)

62. Jesus grants a dead man life

Jesus went with his disciples to a town called Nain. A great number of people went with him. As he came to the gate of the town they met a funeral procession: a young man was being carried out for burial, the only son of his mother. She was a widow and now she was quite alone. Her neighbours and friends were going with her to the grave.

Jesus saw the woman and felt sorry for her. Do not cry, he said. Then he went up and put his hand on the bier. The bearers stood still. Jesus said to the young man: I tell you to get up. And the dead man sat up and began to talk. And Jesus gave him back to his mother.

All those who were present were filled with awe and praised God, saying: A great prophet is working among us; God himself is helping his people. The news about what Jesus was doing for men was spread throughout the land. (Lk 7, 11-17)

63. Why are you afraid?

One evening Jesus said to his disciples: Let us cross over to the other side of the lake. They got into the boat and set out. Suddenly a great storm began raging over the sea. The waves grew higher and the boat began to fill with water. But Jesus was still sleeping in the back of the boat. His disciples woke him and said: Master, do you not care? We are going to perish!

Then Jesus got up. He rebuked the wind and said to the sea: Quiet now! Be calm! And the wind dropped and all was calm again. Then Jesus said to his disciples: Why are you so frightened? Why do you have no faith? The disciples were filled with awe and said to one another: Is he more than just a man? Even the wind and the waves obey him! (Mk 4, 35-41)

64. The hungry are fed

Jesus wanted to be alone with his apostles. But the people followed him everywhere. Jesus spoke to the people about the life that God gives. He cured all those who were in need of his help. In the evening the Twelve came to him and said: Send the people into the villages so that they can find shelter and something to eat. Here it is as lonely as in the desert. But Jesus answered: Give them something to eat yourselves. But they said:

We only have five loaves and two fishes. We would have to go first and buy food for all these people. There were around five thousand men there, as well as women and children.

But Jesus said: Get them to sit in groups of about fifty. The disciples did as Jesus had ordered them. Jesus took the five loaves and the two fishes. He raised his eyes to heaven and blessed the loaves and the fishes. Then he broke them and gave them to his disciples to distribute among the crowd. All those who were there ate and were satisfied. And there was even some bread left over: twelve baskets full. (Lk 9, 10-17)

65. Bread of Life

The people who had eaten the loaves said to each other: This really is the prophet that God is to send into the world. Jesus knew that they wanted to force him to become their king. So he withdrew to be by himself.

The next day they came to Capernaum to look for

him. They found him and asked: When did you come here? Jesus answered: I know you are only looking for me because you were given the bread and could eat your fill. But do not toil for bread that cannot last. Strive for the other bread that brings you eternal life.

Then they asked: What does God want of us? Jesus said: God wants only one thing: that you believe the One he has sent. I am the bread that gives life. Whoever stays close to me will never be hungry again. He who believes in me will never thirst again. (Jn 6)

66. The disciples profess their faith

Jesus was praying in a lonely place. His disciples were with him. Then he asked them: Who do people say that I am? They replied: Some say you are John the Baptist; others say Elijah or one of the other prophets has come back. And what about you? asked Jesus, who do you think I am? Then Peter spoke up: We believe that you are the Messiah, the Redeemer whom God has promised.

Jesus forbade his disciples to tell anyone about this. He said: The Son of Man is destined to suffer grievously. He will be rejected by the elders, the chief priests and the scholars of Holy Scripture. He will be put to death. But on the third day he will be raised up again. Jesus was referring to himself. (Lk 9, 18-22)

67. The witness of the Father

Jesus took Peter, James and John with him up a mountain, in order to pray. As he prayed the appearance of his face was changed and his clothing became brilliant as lightning. Suddenly two men, Moses and Elijah, were there, talking to him. They were bathed in a heavenly light. The two men were speaking with Jesus about what he was to undergo in Jerusalem, in fulfilment of God's will.

Peter and the other two apostles had fallen asleep.

They woke up and saw Jesus, clothed in brightness. They also saw the two men who were with him. As the two were about to leave, Peter said: Master, we are happy here. Let us make three tents, one for you, one for Moses and one for Elijah. He did not know what he was saying. As he spoke, a heavy, dark cloud descended and covered the mountain. The disciples were overcome with fear. And a voice came from the cloud, saying: This is my Son, the Chosen One. Listen to him. When the voice fell silent they saw only Jesus. At that time, the disciples told no one what they had witnessed on the mountain (Lk 9, 28-36)

JESUS TEACHES:
ON LIFE WITH GOD
AND OUR FELLOW MEN

68. To whom does God grant eternal life?

A lawyer - an expert in the Law of Moses - tried to put Jesus to the test. He asked him: What must I do to inherit eternal life? Jesus asked: What is written about it in the Scriptures? The lawyer replied: You must love the Lord your God with all your heart, with all your will, with all your strength. And also, love your neighbour as yourself. You have answered rightly, said Jesus. Do this, and eternal life is yours.

The man wanted to justify himself and said to Jesus: But who is my neighbour?

Then Jesus said: There was once a man, on his way from Jerusalem to Jericho, who was attacked by robbers. They took all he had, beat him and left him lying half dead. A priest came by on the same road. He saw the injured man, and continued on his way. Then a levite came by, saw him, and did not stop. Finally a man from Samaria - a foreigner - came by. He saw the wounded man and took pity on him. He went up and

cleaned and bandaged his wounds. Then he put the man on his own horse and took him to an inn. There he looked after him. Before he rode on the next morning, he gave the innkeeper some money and said: Look after him; on my way back I will repay any extra expense you may have.

Jesus asked the lawyer: What do you think? Which of the three proved himself a neighbour to that man? He replied: The one who took pity on him. Jesus said to him: Go, and do the same yourself. (Lk 10, 25-37)

69. Whom will God admit into his Kingdom?

Jesus said: When the Son of Man returns he will summon all peoples. He will judge men and separate them one from another, as the shepherd separates sheep from goats. Some he will place on his right, the rest on his left.

Then he will say to those on his right: Come, the Father blesses you! You shall live in his kingdom which was prepared for you from the beginning. When I was hungry, you gave me food; when I was thirsty, you gave me drink. When I was without house and home, you made me welcome. When I was naked, you clothed me. When I was sick you visited me. When I was in prison, you came to see me. Then all those standing on his right will ask: Lord, when did we do all these things? And he will reply: I tell you solemnly, whatever you did to the least of my brethren, you did to me.

To those standing on his left he will say: whatever you did not do to the least of my brethren, you did not do to me.

70. The rich farmer's mistake

Jesus warned all those who were with him: Take care and be on your guard that you do not become greedy. For not even a rich man can make his life

secure. And he told them a parable: There was a rich man who had a good harvest from his land. He thought to himself: What shall I do? I do not have enough room to store all my crops. Then he decided: I will pull down my barns and build bigger ones. I will store all my grain and my other goods in them. Then I will be safe and can say to myself: Now I have taken good care of myself. These supplies will last for many years to come. I can eat and drink and have a good time. But God said to the man: You are a fool! This very night you will die. And this hoard of yours, what good will it be to you then? Jesus said: This is what happens when a man stores up treasure for himself, instead of making himself rich in the sight of God. (Lk 12, 15-21)

71. The lost sheep

Many tax-collectors and sinners came to Jesus. They listened to him. This irritated the scribes and pharisees. They complained: This man keeps company with sinners! He even eats with them.

So Jesus told them this parable: Imagine that someone has a hundred sheep. Now if one of the sheep got lost, would he not leave the other ninety-nine grazing and go searching for the lost one until he found it? And when he found it, he would be overjoyed. He would carry it home on his shoulders. Then he would say to his friends and neighbours : rejoice with me, for I have found my lost sheep! And that is how it is with God in heaven, said Jesus. He rejoices over every sinner who changes his life. (Lk 15, 1-7)

72. The Good Shepherd

Jesus said: I am the good shepherd. The good shepherd is always ready to die for his sheep. A shepherd

who works only for money runs away when he sees the wolf coming. Then the wolf can attack and scatter his sheep. He flees because he is only interested in his pay - and has no concern for the sheep. I am the good shepherd. I know my sheep and they know me. And I am ready to die for my sheep.

The Jews who heard this speech disagreed among themselves. Some said: An evil spirit is speaking in him. He does not know what he is saying. Others said: A possessed man does not speak the way he does. How can an evil spirit heal a sick man ? (Jn 10, 11-14; 19-21)

73. A father and his sons

Jesus said: A man had two sons. The younger one said: Father, give me my share of the inheritance. So the father divided his possessions between them. The younger one took everything he had inherited and left for a far country. He wanted to enjoy life and carelessly squandered his money. When he had spent everything, a severe famine broke out. The young man began to feel the pinch. He went to a farmer and asked him for work. The farmer sent him out to a field to care for his pigs. He was starving and would willingly have eaten the husks which the pigs were given. But no one gave him anything. Then he came to his senses and reasoned: My father has many hired workers. They have enough to eat. Before I die here of hunger, I will mend my ways and go back to my father. I will say to him: Father, I have sinned against God and against you. Employ me as one of your hired workers.

His father saw him coming while he was still a long way off. He was moved with pity for his son, ran out to meet him and embraced him. Then his son said: Father, I have sinned against God and against you. So I no longer deserve to be your son. But the father said: Let us prepare a feast and rejoice. My son was dead, now he is alive again. He was lost, now he has returned home.

As the elder son came back from the fields, he heard the music and merriment. He asked a servant: What is going on? The servant replied : Your brother has come home. Your father is having a feast, because he has his son back. Then the elder son was angry and refused to go in. His father came out to explain. But his son reproached him: All these years I have worked for you, yet you never even gave me so much as a kid, so that I could celebrate with my friends. The father said: You are my son. You are with me always and all that I have is yours. But today we can only celebrate and rejoice, because your brother was dead and has come to life. He was lost, and now he has returned home. (Lk 15,11-32)

74. The beggar and the rich man

Once there was a rich man. He used to dress in expensive clothes and had everything he desired. At his gate sat a poor man called Lazarus. Lazarus was in a pitiful state. He had sores all over his body. He was so hungry that he would have gladly eaten the scraps that fell from the rich man's table. Stray dogs harassed him and licked his sores.

When Lazarus died, an angel came and brought him to Abraham in heaven. The rich man also died and was buried. He suffered great torment in the world of the dead. When he looked up he saw Abraham. He also saw Lazarus, safe in Abraham's bosom. So he cried out: Father Abraham, have pity on me. Send Lazarus to me. Let him dip the tip of his finger in water and cool my tongue, for I am in agony in this fire. But Abraham replied: Call to mind your life! You always had whatever you wanted. With Lazarus it was the other way round. So now he is being comforted. There is a great gulf between us and you. No one can cross from here to you, or from you to us.

The rich man implored: I beg you Father, send Lazarus to my parents' house. He should warn my five brothers, so that they do not end up in this place of torment too. Abraham replied: They have Moses and the prophets; let them listen to them. The rich man repeated his plea: Certainly, they have Moses and the prophets, but if someone would come to them from the dead, they would change their lives. But Abraham replied: If they will not listen to Moses and the prophets, they will not be convinced even if someone should rise from the dead. (Lk 16, 19-31)

75. The Pharisee and the tax collector

Once Jesus met some pharisees. They were of the opinion that they observed all of God's commandments and could thus look down on other people. Jesus told them the following story:

Two men went up to the temple to pray. One was a pharisee, the other a tax-collector. The pharisee went to the front and prayed: God, I thank you that I am better than the others. I am faithful to my wife and I am not like that tax-collector over there. I do not steal or cheat. I fast twice a week and give a tenth of all I earn to the temple.

The tax-collector stood at the back. He lowered his head, beat his breast and prayed: God, I am a sinner, have mercy on me. Jesus said: Yes, I tell you, this man went home having been forgiven by God. The other did not. (Lk 18, 9-14)

76. A blind man believes

Jesus drew near to the city of Jericho. There, a blind man sat by the roadside begging. When he noticed that more people than usual were passing by, he asked: What is happening? They told him: Jesus of

Nazareth is coming to the city. The blind man began to shout: Jesus, Son of David! Have pity on me! The people going in front of Jesus scolded him: Hold your tongue! Be quiet! But he cried out all the louder: Son of David! Have pity on me!

Jesus stopped and had the blind man brought to him. When he stood before him, Jesus asked: What do you want me to do for you? The blind man said: Lord I would like to see again. Jesus said: You can see. Your faith has healed you. From that moment on, the blind man could see. He went with Jesus and praised God. All the other people there praised God too. (Lk 18, 35-43)

77. Zacchaeus amends his life

Jesus was walking through Jericho. Zacchaeus lived there. He was a senior tax-collector and a very rich man. He dearly wanted to see Jesus, but the

crowd would not let him through. Zacchaeus was a small man. So he ran on ahead to a place which Jesus had to pass. He climbed a sycamore tree. When Jesus reached the spot he halted, looked up and said: Zacchaeus, come down! I want to stay at your house today.

Zacchaeus climbed down quickly from the tree. He was glad that Jesus wanted to be his guest. But the others who saw this were indignant: He has gone to stay with a sinner. But Zacchaeus said to Jesus: Lord, I will give half my property to the poor. If I have cheated anybody I will give him back four times the amount. Jesus said to him: Today you and your family have seen that God saves. For I have come to seek out and save those who were lost. (Lk 19, 1-10)

DIED - BURIED - RISEN

78. Jesus comes to Jerusalem for the Passover

A few days before the feast of the Passover, Jesus said to the twelve apostles: Now we are going to go up to Jerusalem. There I will be delivered into the hands of the chief priests and scribes. They will condemn me to death and hand me over to the Romans. They will mock me, spit on me, scourge me and then kill me. But after three days I will rise again. (Mk 10, 32-34)

When they were drawing near to the city Jesus sent two disciples on ahead: Go into the village. There you will see a young donkey which nobody has yet ridden. Untie it and bring it to me. If anyone asks you: What are you doing there? tell them: The Lord requires the animal, he will return it shortly. The two entered the village and found everything as Jesus had said. They brought the animal to Jesus.

Jesus rode the donkey into Jerusalem. The people who were going along the road with them spread

their cloaks before Jesus like a carpet of honour. They tore branches from bushes and spread them on the road. The crowd accompanying Jesus cried out: Hosanna! Blessed is he who comes in the name of God. Blessed be the kingdom of our father David. Now it is really coming into existence. Hosanna in the highest! (Mk 11, 1-10)

79. The disciple Judas betrays his Master

Two days before the Passover feast, the chief priests and scribes met together. They were looking for an opportunity to capture Jesus through a trick and kill him. They said to each other: It must not happen during the feast otherwise the people might revolt!

One of the twelve apostles, Judas Iscariot, went to the priests and said: I am prepared to betray Jesus into your hands. They were glad to hear this and promised to give him a reward - thirty pieces of silver. From then on, Judas kept looking for a good moment to betray Jesus. (Mk 14, 1-2. 10-11)

80. The Last Supper

On the day that the Jews slaughter the Passover lamb, Jesus said to Peter and John: Go into the city. There you will meet a man carrying a water jar. Follow him until he enters a house. Ask the master of the house in my name: Where is the room in which I can eat the meal with my disciples? He will show you the room. They both went and found everything as Jesus had said. They prepared the Passover meal.

In the evening Jesus sat at the table with his apostles. He said: I have dearly longed to eat this Passover meal with you before I suffer. I tell you: I will not eat of it again until the Kingdom of God has come about. And he took the bread, gave thanks, broke it, gave it to his disciples and said: Take this and eat it, all of you. This is my Body which will be given up for you.

When supper was ended, he took the cup. Again he gave thanks, gave the cup to his disciples and said: Take this, all of you, and drink from it. This is the cup of my Blood, the Blood of the new and everlasting Covenant. It will be shed for you and for all, so that sins may be forgiven. Do this in memory of me. (Lk 22, 7-20)

81. The true sign of a disciple of Jesus

During the meal Jesus showed his disciples how much he loved them - and how they should love one another. Jesus stood up and tied a towel around his waist. Then he filled a basin with water and began to wash the feet of his disciples. Simon Peter did not want to accept this service. He protested: You, Lord, want to wash my feet? Jesus replied: Only later will you understand what I am doing to you today. Peter

held him off: You shall never wash my feet. But Jesus said: If I do not do this service for you, you do not belong to me. Then Peter said: Lord, then wash not only my feet but also my hands and head.

Later, when Jesus was again sitting at the table, he said: Do you understand what I have done to you? You call me Teacher and Lord. And you are right in doing so. I am your Lord and Teacher. And so, just as I have washed your feet, you also should serve one another and wash one another's feet. I have given you an example. Love one another! You should love one another as I have loved you. That must be how you are recognised: If you love one another, everyone will know that you are my disciples. The greatest love is when a man dies for his friends. You are my friends. Do as I ask.

Jesus said: I will not be with you much longer. But do not be afraid. Believe in God and believe in me. I am going to the Father. There I will prepare a place for you. Then I will come again and take you with me.

You will be with me for ever. I will ask the Father to send you a mighty helper, the Holy Spirit. He is the Spirit of Truth. He will remind you of everything I have told you. (Jn 13-15)

82. Jesus prays on the Mount of Olives

After supper, Jesus went to a garden on the Mount of Olives. His disciples went with him. When they arrived there, Jesus said to them: Pray that you may remain strong in time of temptation. Then he entered the garden alone. He knelt down and prayed: Father, if you will, you can spare me this suffering and death. Nevertheless, not my will, but yours, be done.

In his agony Jesus prayed so intensely that his sweat fell to the earth like drops of blood. Finally he stood up and returned to his disciples. They were asleep because fear and worry had made them tired. Jesus said to them: How can you sleep? Wake up and

pray that you remain steadfast during the coming trial.

While Jesus was still speaking to his disciples, a group of men made their way into the garden. They were led by Judas Iscariot. He drew near to Jesus and was about to kiss him. Jesus asked: Judas, do you want to betray me with this kiss? When the disciples realised that these men had come to arrest Jesus and lead him away, they asked: Lord, should we defend you? One of them drew his sword and cut off the right ear of the High Priest's servant. But Jesus restrained them: Stop this! He touched the ear of the injured man and healed him. Then he said to those who had come to arrest him: You have brought swords and clubs in order to capture me. Was I not with you in the temple day after day? Why did you not venture to lay hands on me then? But this is your hour; this is the reign of darkness. (Lk 22, 39-53)

83. Peter denies the Lord

The abductors arrested Jesus and lead him away to the house of the High Priest. Peter waited for a while and then followed at a distance. A fire was burning in the courtyard and Peter sat down among those warming themselves at the fire. A maid saw Peter and recognised him: Aren't you are one of those who follow Jesus? But Peter denied this and said: I do not know him. Soon someone else recognised him. You are one of Jesus' disciples! Peter denied it again: No, I certainly am not!

About an hour later a third person said: You were with him, you also come from Galilee. Peter insisted: I do not know what you are talking about. At that moment a cock crowed. And Peter remembered what Jesus had said to him earlier: Before the cock crows in the morning, you will deny me three times. Peter stood up and went out. He wept bitterly. (Lk 22, 54-62)

84. Jesus before the high assembly

In the morning the elders of the people, including the chief priests and scribes, assembled. They had Jesus brought in and demanded: If you are the Saviour whom God has promised his people, then tell us. Jesus answered: Even if I were to tell you - you would not believe me! And if I were to ask you - you would not give me an answer. But from now on the Son of Man will sit at the right hand of God. Then they asked him: So you are the Son of God? Jesus replied: You yourselves have said it - I am. They all exclaimed: Now we need no further witnesses against him. We have all heard what he has said. (Lk 22, 66-71)

85. The hearing before Pilate

The leaders of the people brought Jesus to the Roman Governor, Pontius Pilate. They accused him,

saying: He is stirring up the people! He claims he is the Saviour, the King! Pilate asked Jesus: Are you a king? Jesus replied: My Kingdom is not of this world. Otherwise my servants would fight for me. I am a king and I have come into the world to give witness to the truth. Everyone who cares for the truth listens to what I say. Then Pilate asked: What is truth?

Pilate said to those who had accused Jesus: I find no reason to declare him guilty. Every year during the feast of the Passover I release one of your prisoners. Should I release the King of the Jews this Passover? But they shouted: Not Jesus! Set Barabbas free! Barabbas was a robber. So Pilate set Barabbas free and ordered Jesus to be scourged. The soldiers made a crown out of thorns and pressed it onto Jesus' head. They hung a purple robe around his shoulders and mocked him: Hail, King of the Jews! And they hit him in the face.

Pilate led Jesus out to his accusers and said: Behold, the man! But they shouted: He should hang on a cross. Pilate said: Then take him and crucify him! I find no reason to condemn him. But they countered: We have a law which says he must die. For he has declared that he is the Son of God. They kept on pressing Pilate until fear overtook him and he condemned Jesus to death on a cross. (Jn 18, 22 - 19, 16)

86. Jesus dies on the Cross

Jesus carried his cross out of the city to a hill called Golgotha. There they nailed him to the cross. Two criminals had been sentenced with him. Their crosses stood to the left and to the right of Jesus' cross. Pilate had an inscription placed at the top of Jesus' cross. It read: This is Jesus of Nazareth, the King of the Jews. The chief priests were annoyed at this and said to Pilate: Change the inscription so that it reads: He claimed to be the King of the Jews. But Pilate was adamant: what I have written remains written.

Four women stood at the foot of Jesus' cross: his mother, his mother's sister, the wife of Clopas, and Mary Magdalene. The disciple whom Jesus loved stood near his mother. When Jesus saw his mother, he said to her: From now on he is your son. And to the disciple he said: From now on she is your mother. From that time the disciple took Mary to his own home and cared for her.

Jesus now knew that he had accomplished everything. He said: It is accomplished. Then he bowed his head and died. (Jn 19, 17-30)

87. Jesus is buried

Joseph of Arimathea was a man of influence. He belonged to the council of Jews, but was also waiting for the dawning of God's Kingdom. In the evening he went to Pilate and asked: Let me take the body of Jesus down from the cross and bury it. Pilate gave

Joseph permission to bury Jesus' body. Joseph bought linen, took the body of Jesus down from the cross, wrapped it in the linen and placed it in a tomb that had been dug out in the rock-face. Then he rolled a large stone in front of the entrance to the tomb. Two women, Mary Magdalene and Mary, the mother of Joset, watched him and saw where he laid the body of Jesus to rest. (Mk 15, 42-47)

88. The message of the angel

When the Sabbath was over, Mary Magdalene, Mary the mother of James, and Salome bought some spices. They wanted to go to the tomb to anoint the body of Jesus. Early in the morning, just as the sun was rising, they came to the tomb. Along the way they asked one another: Who will remove the stone from the entrance to the tomb for us?

But when they came to the grave they saw that the stone had already been rolled aside. The women en-

tered the tomb and saw a man clothed in white garments sitting on the right side. They were seized with fear. But the angel said to them: Do not be afraid! You are looking for Jesus of Nazareth who died on the cross. He is not here. He is risen. Look, here is the place where his body lay. Go back and tell his disciples, above all Peter, that he is going ahead of you to Galilee. There you will see him as he promised you. The women turned round and fled from the tomb, trembling with awe. They told nobody about what had happened because they were afraid. (Mk 16, 1-8)

89. Two disciples encounter the Risen Lord

That same day two disciples were on their way from Jerusalem to Emmaus. As they walked they spoke about everything they had just lived through in Jerusalem. Then Jesus came and joined them. But the two disciples did not recognise him. He asked them: What are you talking about? Full of sadness, the two disciples halted. One of them, Cleopas, asked: Are you really unaware of what has happened in Jerusalem? The stranger replied: What do you mean?

The two disciples gave their account: We are talking about Jesus of Nazareth. He was a prophet. He preached and worked in a mighty way before God and men. He was condemned to death and executed. We had hoped that he was the Redeemer. And now it is the third day since all this happened. Early this morning, a few women from the circle of his disciples went to the tomb. They did not find his body. They claim they saw an angel and that this messenger of God told them that Jesus was alive. After this a few disciples went to the tomb. They found everything just as the women had said. But they did not see Jesus himself.

At this the stranger said to the two disciples: Do you not understand what is happening? Do you not have any trust in the words of the prophets? The

Messiah had to suffer all this so that God might give him honour, power and life. And he explained to them what was written in Holy Scripture about the Messiah. Finally the three wanderers arrived at the village of Emmaus. Jesus turned around as if he wanted to go on. But the two disciples insisted: Stay with us! It will soon be evening. The day is coming to an end.

Jesus accompanied them into the house and remained with them. Later, as he was sitting with them at the table, he took the bread. He said the prayer of praise, broke the bread and gave it to them. At that moment their eyes were opened and they recognised the Lord. But then they saw him no more. The two disciples said to one another: were not our hearts burning within us as he explained to us the meaning of God's Word?

That same night the two disciples set out and returned to Jerusalem. There the eleven apostles were gathered with many disciples. They said to the two disciples: It is true! The Lord is risen! He has appeared to Peter. Thereupon the two disciples described what they had experienced along the road to Emmaus and how they had recognised Jesus when he broke the bread for them. (Lk 24, 13-35)

90. Encounter in Jerusalem

The disciples had gathered in Jerusalem. They were afraid, and so they had locked the doors. Suddenly Jesus was in their midst and said: Peace be with you. Then he showed them the wounds in his hands. When the disciples recognised their Lord they were full of joy. Then Jesus said to them a second time: Peace be with you. As the Father has sent me, so I am sending you. He said to them: Receive the Holy Spirit. For those whose sins you remit, they are remitted by God; for those whose sins you do not remit, they are not remitted. (Jn 20, 19-23)

91. The Lord sends his messengers
out to all nations

The eleven apostles went to Galilee, to the mountain where Jesus had summoned them. There they saw Jesus. They fell down before him. But some of them had doubts about Jesus. Jesus came up and said: My Father has given me authority - over heaven and over the earth. And with this authority I am sending you. Go out to all the nations. Make all people into my disciples. Baptise them in the name of the Father, the Son and the Holy Spirit. Teach them and tell them everything, so that they can live in the way that I have shown you. You may be sure of this: I will not leave you alone. I will be with you all days, until the end of time. (Mt 28, 16-20)

JESUS IS STILL WITH US

92. Farewell to the disciples

Forty days had passed since Easter. During this time the Lord appeared to his disciples. He told them: Stay in Jerusalem and wait for the Helper whom the Father will send. John baptised with water in the Jordan. You will be baptised with the Holy Spirit. Then you will be my witnesses. Here in Jerusalem and in all countries, as far as the ends of the earth.

After he had said all this to his disciples he was lifted up into the sky. A cloud came and concealed him. The disciples stared spellbound into the sky. But then two men in white garments were there with them. They said: Why are you standing there gazing into the sky? Jesus, who has departed from you into heaven, will come again. You will recognise him. (Acts 1, 1-11)

93. God's new people: The Church of Jesus Christ

On the day of Pentecost all the disciples of Jesus, both men and women, as well as Mary, his mother, were gathered together in the same house. They were waiting for the Helper whom Jesus had promised them. Then suddenly there came from heaven a roaring sound like a mighty wind. It filled the whole house. Tongues of fire appeared and descended upon each one of them. They were all filled with the Holy Spirit. They praised God, and they praised his Son, Jesus Christ.

Many people from distant lands had come to Jerusalem for the feast. A large crowd thronged in front of the house where the disciples were staying. They were all filled with awe, for each of them heard the disciples of Jesus speaking in his own language. They were

perplexed and asked each other: What does this mean? Then Peter began to speak. He called out: Listen to me! I will explain it to you. What the prophet Joel foretold in the name of God is being fulfilled here and now: At the end of time God pours out his Spirit on all mankind. Remember Jesus of Nazareth. He came by the will of God and did the deeds of God. You witnessed this yourselves. God gave his own Son - you accused him and had him condemned by the Romans. He died on the cross, but God raised him up from the dead. We are all his witnesses. God has exalted him. He is the Messiah.

The words of Peter went to the hearts of many people. They asked: Brothers, what are we to do? Peter replied: Change your lives. Be baptised in the name of Jesus Christ for the forgiveness of your sins. Then he will send you the Holy Spirit. Many listened to Peter and were baptised. That one day three thousand people joined the community of Jesus Christ. (Acts 2)

94. Living for Jesus - dying for him

From now on the apostles worked in Jerusalem. They healed the sick and gave witness to the life and death of Jesus. More and more people came to believe. The high priests and the teachers of Israel wanted people to forget Jesus. So they arrested the apostles, questioned them and forbade them to teach in the name of Jesus. But the apostles did not pay attention to this prohibition. Stephen, one of the first deacons, was stoned to death. But before he collapsed under the hail of stones he called out: I see heaven is open. I see the Son of Man, he is standing at the right hand of God. Lord Jesus, take me!

The community of Jesus was persecuted in Jerusalem. All those who acknowledged their faith were driven out of the city. But wherever they went they proclaimed what God had done for people through Jesus Christ. And in all these places they founded new communities. (Acts 2 - 8)

95. Paul - Apostle to the Nations

Paul was a devout Jew. He was very well versed in Holy Scriptures and was convinced that Jesus was not the Saviour, but had seduced the people. So Paul went from town to town punishing those who were loyal to Jesus and trying to make them abandon their faith in him. As he was riding towards Damascus to track down the Christians there and bring them to Jerusalem as captives, he had an experience which changed his whole life. Blinding light from heaven surrounded him. He fell to the ground and heard a voice saying: Why are you persecuting me?

Paul did not know what was happening to him. He asked: Who are you, Lord? And he heard the answer: I am Jesus, and you are persecuting me. Get up! Go into the city. There you will find out what you have to do. Paul went to Damascus. There he met Ananias, a disciple. Ananias refused to believe that Paul had encountered the Lord and had become a disciple. But the Lord said to him: I have chosen Paul. He has to see to it that all nations know my name. At that Ananias accepted Paul into the community.

From then on Paul no longer persecuted Christians but preached about Christ instead. In Damascus and in the other cities he proclaimed Jesus Christ as the Saviour. He became a wandering preacher and spoke in the synagogues of the Jews. He founded Christian communities. He did all he could so that Jews and Greeks, and people of all the nations of the earth might belong to the new people of God.

Paul was persecuted and hunted from one town to the next, even as far as Greece. He wrote letters to the communities which he had founded. In these letters he admonishes and encourages them. He explains what faith in Jesus Christ means to men, and what it is to live as a Christian. In the end Paul was arrested in Jerusalem and sent to Rome as a prisoner. There he was condemned and put to death. He died for Jesus Christ. (Acts 9 - 28)

96. Paul writes to the Christian Communities

Jesus died, he was raised from the dead and sits enthroned at God's right hand. He intercedes for us. So now, can anything separate us from the love of Christ? Affliction or distress, hunger or cold, persecution or death? We overcome all these things because he loves us. I am certain of this: no power in the world can separate us from him. (Rom 9, 35-39)

You believe in Jesus Christ and thus you are sons and daughters of God. You have been baptised and so you belong to the community of Christ. In this community it no longer matters whether you are Jew or Greek, slave or free, man or woman, for you are all one in Christ. (Gal 3, 26-28)

Be happy at all times. Do not cease praying. Be thankful for everything. This is what God expects of

those who profess Jesus Christ. Be open to what the Spirit tells you. Test all things - retain what is good. Keep away from evil. (1 Thess 5, 16-22)

The love of Christ overwhelms us. For we have learned: One man died for all men so that those living should live no longer for themselves, but for the one who died for them and was raised to life. (2 Cor 5, 14-15)

Dear brothers! Rejoice and accept admonishment, do not quarrel with one another and live in peace! Then the God of love and peace will be with you. The grace of Jesus Christ, the Lord, the love of God and the fellowship of the Holy Spirit be with you all. (2 Cor 13, 11.13)

97. We do not live like people who have no hope

God gives life. All living things have life through him. But our life lasts only seventy years, or eighty for those who are strong. Most of these are hardship and sorrow. It is over quickly, like the flight of a bird. (Ps 90, 10)

All men must die. They ask: Is death stronger than God? But those who believe are sure that God's life is stronger than death. His love abandons no one. One man expresses in a prayer what many people hope for: You do not surrender me to the underworld, nor allow the one who trusts you to lie in the grave for ever. You show me the path to life. In you I find fullness of joy. Your right hand is good to me for evermore. (Ps 16, 10-11)

The apostle Paul writes: Brothers, do not grieve over your dead as do those, who have no hope. For if Jesus himself died and rose again - which we firmly believe - then, through Jesus and with Jesus, God will bring the dead to himself. (1 Thess 4, 13-14)

Israel's prophets speak of the 'Day of the Lord'. They refer to the day when all earthly powers will pass away because God will come to gather his people together and begin his reign. The 'Day of the Lord' is the 'Last Day' of our passing world. On that day God will transform creation along with its structures of injustice, sin and suffering: On that day the heavens will dissolve in fire and the elements will melt in the flames. What we look forward to then is what God has promised - a new heaven and a new earth, where justice dwells. (2 Peter 3, 12-13)

The disciples of Jesus are impatient. They ask him: Tell us, when will the Kingdom of God begin? Jesus replies: Nobody knows the day or the hour; not even the angels in heaven. The Son also does not know, just the Father alone. (Mt 24, 36; Mk 13, 32)

But there is one thing you may do: Stay alert, because you do not know the day when your Master is coming. (Mt 24, 42)

When the Lord of creation comes to bring it to completion, he will stand in judgement over the living and the dead. At this judgement mankind will recognise that there is only one Lord and only one love. They will realise that there is only one misfortune - that of being excluded from his fellowship; and only one joy - that of living in his presence.

The apostle Paul writes: God has not destined us for the wrath of his judgement but that we may attain Salvation, through Jesus Christ Our Lord. He died for us so that we might live united with him. (1 Thess 5, 9-10)

Jesus says to a father who is mourning his dead child: Do not be afraid; only have faith. (Mk 5, 36)

98. God's new world

The seer John beholds God's new world. He writes: I saw a new heaven and a new earth. The first heaven, the old earth and also the sea were no more. I saw the New Jerusalem coming down from God out of heaven. And I heard a loud voice calling out: See, from now on God lives among men. They will be his people and he will remain with them for ever. He will wipe away every tear from their eyes. There will be no more death, nor mourning, nor crying, nor distress. For what previously was, has passed away. And the One who was sitting on the throne spoke: See, now I am making all things new. Yes! Come Lord Jesus! (Rev 21, 1-5)

INDEX

FROM THE BOOKS OF THE OLD TESTAMENT

FROM THE BOOKS OF THE NEW TESTAMENT